A Passion
for Partnering
with God

Study Guide based on

Mover of Men and Mountains

The Autobiography of R.G. LeTourneau

13 Studies for Groups or Individuals
by David Carpenter

Wisdom Cries Out Publications
Cypress, TX
www.wisdomcriesout.com

First Edition, September 2011
Copyright © 2010 by David Carpenter

Permission to use quotations from *Mover of Men and Mountains*, the Autobiography of R.G. LeTourneau, obtained from Moody Publishers, Chicago, Illinois. www.moodypublishers.com

Historical Events timeline information researched on Wikipedia:
Wikipedia: The Free Encyclopedia. Wikimedia Foundation, Inc. December 2010. http://en.wikipedia.org

Scripture taken from the NEW AMERICAN STANDARD BIBLE®,
Copyright © 1960,1962,1963,1968,1971,1972,1973,1975,1977,1995
by The Lockman Foundation. Used by permission.

Photos in the Study Guide were provided by Dale Hardy of the R.G. LeTourneau Heritage Center.

Cover Artwork © oconner - Fotolia.com

ISBN-13: 978-1456470227
ISBN-10: 1456470221

Contents

A Passion for Partnering with God

Introduction to this Study Guide

God needs businessmen as partners as well as preachers. When He created the world and everything in it, He didn't mean for us to stop there and say, "God, you've done it all. There's nothing left for us to build." He wanted us to take off from there and really build for His greater glory.

Mover of Men and Mountains, R.G. LeTourneau, Moody Publishers, 1967, Page 1

R.G. LeTourneau lived his life as an engineer, entrepreneur, and evangelist in partnership with God. His remarkable story is told, in his own words, in "Mover of Men and Mountains." This study guide is designed to accompany you through this amazing autobiography. The study guide presents questions for all 26 chapters. The questions are grouped to form 13 lessons, two book chapters for each study guide lesson.

The guide focuses on **Five Major Themes** that run throughout the book. Every study question is labeled to link it to one of the five major themes.

PASSION – R.G. had a deep passion for machines and large equipment. This passion was displayed through his mechanical engineering genius, which led to 299 U.S. patents.*

PROJECTS – Beyond mechanical machinery, R.G. developed many production systems, factories, and several manufacturing sites which were combined with educational campuses. Behind every project was a desire to increase human productivity.

PAIN – In his autobiography R.G. recounts no less than 9 significant illnesses, injuries, or "near death" incidents. His reaction to these painful situations reveals much about the man and his enduring strength.

PATH – God's path for our lives is never as straight or simple as we might desire. God led R.G. on a life path through many turbulent times, challenging relationships, and a multi-faceted career development program.

PARTNERING WITH GOD – Clearly the main theme of the book, and R.G.'s life, is his commitment to partnering with God. The ever-developing partnership drastically changed his perspective from the temporary to the eternal. This partnership led him to become a prolific speaker and author, neither of which were his "natural" gifts.

Each lesson includes several sections, beyond just study questions. There are historical highlights for the years covered by each chapter. The "Secrets of Scripture" section relates R.G.'s writings to the truth of God's Word. The "Secrets of Success" section highlights nuggets of truth taught by R.G. that are "hidden" throughout the book.

* http://www.letu.edu/about_LU/museum/Museum_Online/the_machines/index.html

A Passion for Partnering with God

Why This Study?

"These are difficult times. The challenges are new, and the dangers ever increasing." To some extent these thoughts are true for every generation. There are always obstacles to overcome, and new frontiers to be conquered.

The story of R.G. LeTourneau is more than just another saga of trials, tribulations, and triumphs. This is a story of enduring hope and persevering passion. As you read R.G.'s autobiography you will have a front row seat into the life, thoughts, and heart of a true American and a true Christian. Through the study questions you will be drawn to a deeper level as you encounter five major themes which are woven throughout R.G.'s life.

The study questions will increase your insight into the relationship between man and machine. You will also clearly see the growing relationship between man and God. And, you will experience the sorrows, heartbreaks, and victories that were the life of R.G. LeTourneau.

How to Benefit From This Study

1. Get involved. Whether you are studying on your own, or in a small group, the best way to learn is to interact with the material. Ask questions about the questions. Take notes. Explore beyond the pages. Jot down your emotions and reactions to both the joys and the sorrows.

2. Reading the book, *Mover of Men and Mountains* is absolutely required for this study. Every question is related directly to the book. And, every question is labeled with the page number(s) addressing that specific question. The page numbers are taken from the 1967, 1972 paperback edition, ISBN: 0-8024-3818-0. The electronic editions of this autobiography will not have the page numbers. Both print and electronic editions are widely available on the Internet.

3. Recommended reading is listed at the end of the study guide. Historical highlights from 1888 to 1959 are given at the beginning of each study. You are encouraged to further your education by also studying the inventors, builders, and leaders who were living during this intriguing time period. You may also be interested in studying more about mechanical engineering, project management, world missions, leadership training, or industrial arts.

4. Incorporate art into your study. "A picture is worth a thousand words." Draw and doodle and sketch. Color in the margins and blank spaces of this study guide. Pictures you draw will help your mind be fully involved in the study. And, pictures will help you remember your thoughts and reactions. Finding and studying pictures of LeTourneau equipment will help you appreciate the size and complexity of these amazing machines.

5. Suggested test questions and additional resources for homeschool families are available at www.wisdomcriesout.com.

R.G. LeTourneau - 1901

Photograph courtesy of R.G. LeTourneau Heritage Center

Caleb and Elizabeth LeTourneau - 1924

Photograph courtesy of R.G. LeTourneau Heritage Center

Study 1

Looking Back
R.G. LeTourneau lived during a time of remarkable transformation. He was born just about 20 years after the Civil War in the United States. He died less than two months before Apollo 11 landed and Neil Armstrong became the first human to walk on the moon. During his lifetime daily travel evolved from horses and wagons to motorcycles, cars, buses, and airplanes.

Looking Ahead
In the first two chapters we see the beginning of R.G.'s life path. Through these chapters we see how God used his family, neighbors, and curiosity to prepare R.G. for many years of partnering with God.

What inventions were discovered in the 20 years before you were born?

How have the inventions of the past 50 years influenced your life?

Which member of your family has had the biggest impact on your life?

Chapter 1 – 1888 - 1889 (Birth to 2 years old; Born on November 30, 1888)
Historical Events in 1888:
- The "Great Blizzard of '88" in New Jersey, New York, Massachusetts and Connecticut kills more than 400 people.
- Kodak trademark is registered by George Eastman. He also receives a patent for his "roll film" camera.
- Grover Cleveland, president in the U.S., is defeated in his re-election bid by Benjamin Harrison.
Historical Events in 1889:
- North Dakota (39th) and South Dakota (40th) gain statehood on November 2.
- Montana (41st) and Washington (42nd) also gain statehood in November.

Chapter 2 – 1890's (Ages 2 to 13)
Historical Events in 1890:
- "The Sleeping Beauty" ballet premieres in St. Petersburg, Russia.
- Idaho (43rd) and Wyoming (44th) gain statehood.
Historical Events in 1892:
- Ellis Island opens to process immigrants.
- First official game of basketball is played at the YMCA in Springfield, Massachusetts.
Historical Events in 1893:
- Rudolf Diesel, living in Berlin, Germany, receives a patent for the diesel engine.
- "The Panic of 1893" sets off a widespread economic depression in the United States.
Historical Events in 1896:
- Utah (45th) gains statehood.
- Gold is discovered in Alaska setting the stage for a gold rush in 1897.
Historical Events in 1898:
- The Spanish-American war begins when the United States declares war on Spain.
- The Hawaiian Islands are annexed by United States.

Watch for these Key Words: partnership, father, cabin boy

Study 1

Chapter 1 – 1888 to 1889

1. What does R.G. mean by "a Christian businessman owes as much to God as a preacher does"? (Page 1, Partnering)

2. What is the value of good machines? (Page 2, Passion)

3. Describe R.G.'s formal education and financial situation. (Pages 2-3, Path)

4. What does it mean to be in a partnership with God? (Page 3, Partnering)

5. Family history:
    Where did R.G.'s grandparents live? (Pages 4-5, Path)

    When was R.G. born? (Page 7, Path)

    Where did the family move in 1890? (Page 8, Path)

Study 1

Chapter 2 – 1890's

6. Describe the relationship between R.G. and his father in his childhood years. (Pages 9-10, Path)

7. What happened when R.G. was in the fifth grade? How did that impact his next year at school, seventh grade? (Pages 11-12, Path)

8. What was the first piece of "earth-moving equipment" he invented? (Page 13, Passion)

9. What accident resulted in the "first of many miracles" in R.G.'s life? (Page 14, Pain)

10. Instead of becoming a "cabin boy," what happened when R.G. ran away from home? (Page 15, Path)

11. How did R.G. and his father resolve their differences? What lesson did R.G. learn that "changed my whole attitude"? (Page 17, Path)

Study 1

Secrets in Scripture

From Chapter 2 we are able to learn a lot about R.G. and his relationship with his father during his childhood. From R.G.'s experience with his dad we can see how a deeper understanding of love changes relationships.

> *By this we know that we love the children of God, when we love God and observe His commandments. For this is the love of God, that we keep His commandments; and His commandments are not burdensome.*
>
> 1 John 5:2-3 (NASB)

The book of Proverbs has much to say about the importance of the father-son relationship.

> *My son, observe the commandment of your father and do not forsake the teaching of your mother;*
> *Bind them continually on your heart; Tie them around your neck.*
> *When you walk about, they will guide you; When you sleep, they will watch over you;*
> *And when you awake, they will talk to you.*
>
> Proverbs 6:20-22 (NASB)

Secrets of Success

R.G. writes about his "single-minded stubbornness" on Page 16. Later in the chapter he identifies himself as "that stubborn LeTourneau kid."

Often times our greatest strengths are also our greatest weaknesses.
How did his stubbornness negatively affect his family relationships?

How might this same stubbornness aid R.G. in overcoming technical and business challenges later in his life?

Famous Inventors – Mid 1800's and Early 1900's

1833 to 1896 - Alfred Nobel (Dynamite, 1866)
1847 to 1922 - Alexander Graham Bell (Telephone, 1876)
1847 to 1931 - Thomas Alva Edison (First commercially practical incandescent light, 1879)
1863 to 1947 - Henry Ford (Automobile Mass Production, 1913)
1867 to 1934 - Madame Curie (Nobel Prize in Physics, 1903 and in Chemistry, 1911)
1865 to 1943 - George Washington Carver (Chemurgy, 1920's)
1879 to 1955 - Albert Einstein ($E = mc^2$, 1905)

R.G. LeTourneau with his mother and siblings - 1927

Photograph courtesy of R.G. LeTourneau Heritage Center

"From the hills back of my friend's home we and thousands of refugees watched the city burn. For several days we got our food by standing in a breadline and taking what they handed to us. I'll never forget that first day – things were looking pretty bad, and there were hundreds of thousands homeless."

R.G. LeTourneau talking about his experience after the San Francisco Earthquake

Ackland, Donald F. *Moving Heaven and Earth.*
New York: The Iversen-Ford Associates, 1949, Page 201

Study 2

Looking Back
In the first study we saw how his family played a big part of R.G.'s early development. How did R.G. and his father get along during R.G.'s boyhood?

What personality characteristic contributed to R.G.'s boyhood struggles?

Looking Ahead
In the next two chapters we see R.G. continue on his life path as God directs him toward a life of invention. Gradually, we see R.G. begin to develop a passion for machines and projects.

What is one thing in life that causes you to strive with passion?

How can passion help us to overcome difficulties?

When does passion become a part of the problem, and not part of the solution?

Chapter 3 – 1902 to 1904 (14 to 16 years old)
Historical Events in 1900:
- The Gold Standard Act establishes gold as only basis for U.S. paper money.
- A hurricane kills approximately 8,000 people in Galveston, Texas.
- Hawaii becomes a U.S. territory.

Historical Events in 1901:
- President William McKinley is assassinated.
- An oil gusher occurs at Spindletop in Beaumont, Texas.

Historical Events in 1903:
- Ford Motor Company is founded by Henry Ford.
- Orville Wright makes his first flight in an aircraft with a petrol engine at Kitty Hawk, North Carolina.

Historical Events in 1904:
- Work begins on the Panama Canal.
- The ice cream cone is invented.

Chapter 4 – 1905 to 1907 (17 to 19 years old)
Historical Events in 1905:
- Theodore Roosevelt is sworn in as president of United States.
- Albert Einstein publishes 4 scientific papers.
- The Wright brothers fly for 39 minutes.

Historical Events in 1906:
- San Francisco earthquake kills at least 3,000 and leaves 300,000 homeless.
- The first radio program is broadcast from Brant Rock, Massachusetts.

Historical Events in 1907:
- 19-year-old Jim Casey and 18-year-old Claude Ryan found the American Messenger Company in Seattle, Washington. The company becomes United Parcel Service (UPS) in 1919.
- Oklahoma (46th) gains statehood.

Watch for these Key Words: "man growed," file, revival, vocational

Study 2

Chapter 3 – 1902 to 1904

1. Being "a man growed" meant that R.G. didn't want to go where anymore? (Page 22, Path)

2. What did his dad arrange for R.G. to do instead? (Page 23, Path)

3. What was R.G.'s first work assignment? (Pages 24-25, Path)

4. What advice did he get from Joe? (Page 25, Path)

5. What were the two "priceless" lessons he learned from Mr. Hill and his file? (Page 26, Projects)

6. In 1902 R.G. learned some important lessons about keeping a business running from Mr. Hill. List some "new tricks" businesses may need to learn in the 2000's. (Page 29, Projects)

7. There was a German machinist who gave R.G. a special project. What was that project? (Pages 30-31, Projects)

8. What were two results of the city-wide revival? (Page 33, Partnering)

Study 2

Chapter 4 – 1905 to 1907

9. What is the first part of the "good lesson" taught by the German mechanic? (Page 36, Path)

10. What was the second part of the lesson, the second "semester"? (Page 38, Path)

11. What happened to the East Portland Iron Works? (Page 39, Path)

12. Why did R.G. like vocational school? (Page 41, Passion)

13. Describe R.G.'s reaction to the surviving the San Francisco earthquake. (Page 42, Pain)

14. What events caused R.G. to move to Oregon? (Pages 44-45, Path)

15. Another "near death" experience in the wilderness of Oregon taught R.G. a lesson about partners, and also formed his opinion of dentists. What were these lessons? (Pages 46-47, Pain)

Study 2

Secrets in Scripture

In Chapter 4 another "near death" experience shakes-up R.G. Years later he tells his audiences that even in frightening times we can trust God, and have "complete confidence in His rightness when His will is done." (Page 42)

> *God is our refuge and strength, A very present help in trouble.*
> *Therefore we will not fear, though the earth should change*
> *And though the mountains slip into the heart of the sea;*
> *Though its waters roar and foam,*
> *Though the mountains quake at its swelling pride. Selah.*
>
> Psalm 46: 1-3 (NASB)

> *Though I walk in the midst of trouble, You will revive me;*
> *You will stretch forth Your hand against the wrath of my enemies,*
> *And Your right hand will save me.*
> *The LORD will accomplish what concerns me;*
> *Your lovingkindness, O LORD, is everlasting;*
> *Do not forsake the works of Your hands.*
>
> Psalm 138:7-8 (NASB)

Secrets of Success

The old German machinist taught R.G. several valuable life-lessons. "To learn something, you must make something." (Page 30) This lesson about getting started influenced R.G. throughout his life. You can see it in his love for vocational education.

Many times the fear of failure keeps us from getting started. But, paraphrasing the words of the R.G.'s mentor, the greatest failure is a failure to start making something.

While working as an apprentice in the foundry R.G. found that "a lot of the old timers resented the changes being made ..." Instead of resisting change, R.G. found that he "was one of the lucky ones trained to accept change *as* routine."

Are you afraid of failing? Are you afraid of change?

What can you do to improve your attitude towards failure and change?

Inside the Stockton Garage

Photograph courtesy of R.G. LeTourneau Heritage Center

R.G. LeTourneau in the Driver's Seat - 1914

This is most likely the car he was riding in during the race track crash.

Photograph courtesy of R.G. LeTourneau Heritage Center

Study 3

Looking Back
Much of what R.G. learned in his teenage years was in the "School of Hard Knocks." With the guidance of some patient teachers, R.G. builds a foundation of mechanical knowledge.

Who were some of his teachers in the classroom of "real life"?

Why are some people afraid to start a new project or study a new subject?

Looking Ahead
In what seems to be a string of completely unrelated events, God begins to add to R.G.'s mechanical foundation. These events expose him to a range of experiences that will make him an excellent project manager.

What is the difference between designing a single product and completing an entire project?

Which area is your personal strength, working on one thing at a time or overseeing several pieces in a larger project?

Chapter 5 – 1908 to 1909 (20 to 21 years old)
Historical Events in 1908:
- The Model T Ford is introduced.
- The Bible Institute of Los Angeles (now Biola University) is founded.

Historical Events in 1909:
- William Taft is inaugurated as the 27th U.S. president.
- National Association for the Advancement of Colored People (NAACP) is founded.
- First races are held at the Indianapolis Motor Speedway.

Chapter 6 – 1910 to 1914 (22 to 26 years old)
Historical Events in 1910:
- Boy Scouts of America is organized by William D. Boyce.
- Henri Coanda exhibits the first non-propeller (jet) plane, the Coanda-1910.

Historical Events in 1911:
- Ray Harroun wins the first Indianapolis "500."
- Italy declares war on the Ottoman Empire which begins the Italo-Turkish War.

Historical Events in 1912:
- The RMS Titanic sinks on its maiden voyage taking the lives of over 1,500 people.
- New Mexico (47th) and Arizona (48th) gain statehood.

Historical Events in 1913:
- The 16th Amendment to the United States Constitution is ratified. (Income Taxes)
- Woodrow Wilson becomes 28th President of the United States.

Historical Events in 1914:
- Austria-Hungary declares war on Serbia to start World War I.
- The Panama Canal opens.

Watch for these Key Words: gold, Stockton, carburetor, racing

Study 3

Chapter 5 – 1908 to 1909

1. What question did R.G. answer to get a job at the Yerba Buena Power System? (Page 49, Path)

2. What skill did R.G. learn that would influence his future products? (Page 50, Path)

3. What lessons did R.G. learn from the gold mine and farm? (Pages 52-53, Path)

4. After cutting his leg, R.G. had a time of self-assessment. What was his conclusion? (Pages 53-54, Pain)

5. After awarding himself a "B.M. degree" the only work R.G. could find was "tending the stationary gasoline engines for a crew building a bridge across the Stanislaus River." This position introduced him to the complexities and frustrations of working on a big project. What are some of the observations R.G. made regarding construction work in 1909? (Page 55, Projects)

6. What town did R.G. drive to after the bridge was finished? (Page 57, Path)

Study 3

Chapter 6 – 1910 to 1914

7. What job was he given at the service station? (Page 59, Path)

8. How does the lesson of the dirty carburetor apply to partnering with God? (Page 61, Partnering)

9. How did R.G. get his $1000 down payment for the new station? (Page 62, Projects)

10. What was the Regal demonstration at the county fair? (Page 63, Projects)

11. Describe R.G.'s injuries due to the racing track crash. (Page 65, Pain)

12. What was the "cure" for the misaligned neck? (Page 66, Pain)

13. What two additional areas of study did R.G. undertake as a result of working on cars and batteries? (Pages 70-71, Path)

Study 3

Secrets in Scripture

The story of the "Dirty Carburetor" is found in Chapter 6. R.G. tells this story to illustrate how a small piece of dirt can impede a large, powerful machine. Many people believe they can allow a small sin to remain in their life. However, for God's power to be complete in our lives, we must admit to, and confront every lingering sin. "Yet the Lord is willing to cleanse you of all sins, large and small if you will only ask Him." (Page 61)

> *If we say that we have no sin, we are deceiving ourselves and the truth is not in us.*
> *If we confess our sins, He is faithful and righteous to forgive us our sins and*
> *to cleanse us from all unrighteousness.*
>
> 1 John 1:8-9 (NASB)

> *Be gracious to me, O God, according to Your lovingkindness;*
> *According to the greatness of Your compassion blot out my transgressions.*
> *Wash me thoroughly from my iniquity*
> *And cleanse me from my sin.*
>
> Psalm 51:1-2 (NASB)

Secrets of Success

During the early working years of R.G.'s life he had many different jobs. Starting with his work on the widow's farm, can you remember all the jobs R.G. held during these first six chapters? (If you need help see Page 54)

What technical or social skill did R.G. pick up from each of these jobs?

In the years ahead God is going to use this wide array of jobs to form a strong foundation for R.G. He will use his mechanical, electrical, and metal knowledge as a basis for his earth-moving designs.

What are some of the experiences, knowledge, and skills in your life that God may be able to use in the future?

Trusting God means allowing Him to lead us and teach us in every situation

Evelyn's Family

Photograph courtesy of R.G. LeTourneau Heritage Center

Evelyn at 18 years old and Caleb at age three months

Photograph courtesy of R.G. LeTourneau Heritage Center

Study 4

Looking Back
In the previous chapter R.G. survived a horrific crash that left him with a broken neck. The misaligned neck was partially restored through a motorcycle accident.

Have you ever experienced an illness or injury that was "life-threatening"?

If you did experience a painful and frightening situation, how did you respond to the hurt and fear?

Looking Ahead
Sadly, the pain in R.G.'s life does not end in Chapter 6. As you read Chapters 7 and 8 you will see another "near-death experience" and more illness. Through these difficult times, R.G.'s faith in God will be severely tested.

How might pain and suffering be a part of God's path for R.G.?

What is the impact of passion when someone faces difficult circumstances?

Chapter 7 – 1915 to 1917 (27 to 29 years old)
Historical Events in 1915:
- The Neon Tube sign is patented by Georges Claude.
- Albert Einstein publishes his "General Theory of Relativity."
- Rocky Mountain Park is established in Colorado.
- A locust plague lasts seven months in Palestine.

Historical Events in 1916:
- The first successful blood transfusion is accomplished using blood that had been stored and cooled.
- President Woodrow Wilson sends troops over the U.S.-Mexico border to pursue Pancho Villa.
- William J. Newton and Morris Goldberg invent the light switch.

Historical Events in 1917:
- U.S. troops withdraw from Mexico.
- U.S. enters World War I.
- Britain declares support of a Jewish "national home" in Palestine in the Balfour Declaration.

Chapter 8 – 1918 (30 years old)
Historical Events in 1918:
- Woodrow Wilson's delivers his "Fourteen Points" speech.
- U.S. Congress authorizes time zones and daylight savings time.
- An influenza pandemic begins, eventually killing 25,000,000 people in 6 months.
- A. M. Nicholson invents the radio crystal oscillator.
- Edwin Armstrong invents the super heterodyne receiver.
- Charles Strite invents the pop-up toaster.

Watch for these Key Words: eloping, sickness, service station

Study 4

Chapter 7 – 1915 to 1917

1. What was R.G.'s first "successful invention"? (Page 72, Passion)

2. Lying under a car, R.G. experiences another near death situation. What happened? (Page 73, Pain)

3. Did R.G. agree with Evelyn's parents in regard to their marriage? (Page 75, Partnering)

4. What were some of the steps R.G. took to avoid detection and allow them to complete their marriage plans? (Pages 76-77, Projects)

5. Since he couldn't serve in the military, where did R.G. work during World War I? (Page 78, Path)

6. What sickness once again brought R.G. to the edge of death? (Page 80, Pain)

Study 4

Chapter 8 – 1918

7. How was the service station business going when he returned to town? (Pages 82-83, Projects)

8. What caused the business troubles? (Page 83 Projects)

9. What was "one of the most valuable experiences in my life"? Why? (Page 84, Path)

10. What sickness infected Caleb? (Pages 84-85, Pain)

11. How did R.G. respond to the outcome? What was God's response? (Page 85, Partnering)

12. Describe the "Christian Missionary Alliance" church. (Pages 87-88, Path)

13. How did God use the Peniel Mission House to change R.G.'s reaction to people in desperate situations, "the derelicts we called winos"? (Page 89, Partnering)

Study 4

Secrets in Scripture

One verse that guided R.G. during his life was Matthew 6:33. Being God's partner means pursuing God's glory above our own interests. When we seek our own glory, we depend on our own resources. When we seek God's kingdom, we can trust in His plan and provision.

Notice how "seeking," "attaining," and "worrying" are related in these verses. Who has more inner peace, someone seeking God's glory, or someone setting out on their own?

> *"But seek first His kingdom and His righteousness, and all these things will be added to you. So do not worry about tomorrow; for tomorrow will care for itself. Each day has enough trouble of its own."*
>
> Matthew 6:33-34 (NASB)

Jesus warned us to seek and serve God with our whole heart, focused on eternal treasure.

> *"Do not store up for yourselves treasures on earth, where moth and rust destroy, and where thieves break in and steal. But store up for yourselves treasures in heaven, where neither moth nor rust destroys, and where thieves do not break in or steal; for where your treasure is, there your heart will be also."*
>
> Matthew 6:19-21 (NASB)

Secrets of Success

Being a partner of God applies to working on machines just as much as it does to working in ministry.

"I was just a mechanic striving to translate His laws in terms of machinery, and as long as I understood I was just His follower, and didn't get to thinking I was operating under my own head of steam, I was on the right track." (Page 79)

"Of course it wasn't my talk that had brought about the reformation. I had merely brought to the attention of these men the power and capacity of our Lord … We can be His instruments, but only God can work the wonders." (Page 89)

How do these quotes apply to being partners with God?

What happens when we choose to be an instrument that does not rely on God?

24

"We in America have enjoyed the highest standard of living of any country on this globe. I firmly believe it is because our forefathers came here seeking freedom to worship God, and God has blessed our land. But I wonder if we haven't been getting away from the God of our forefathers. I wonder if we haven't been worshipping the almighty dollar more than the Almighty God, Who made this world and all the dollars that are in it. I wonder if what this country needs isn't to go back to the God of our forefathers and seek Him first."

R.G. LeTourneau on how God has blessed America.

Lorimer, Albert W. *God Runs My Business: The Story of R.G. LeTourneau*. New York: Fleming H. Revell Company, 1941, Pages 174-175

Restored 1917 Holt Tractor – Picture taken in 2004

Photograph courtesy of R.G. LeTourneau Heritage Center

Study 5

Looking Back

Partnering with God means trusting God in any, and every, situation. Unfortunately, at this point in his life R.G. likes to take things into his own hands. We saw an example of that in Chapter 7 and the wedding plans.

When is it more difficult to trust completely in God, when there is trouble, or when life is great?

How did pain stretch R.G.'s commitment to partnering with God?

Looking Ahead

World War I comes to an end in 1919. R.G. continues on his path to learning about machines and making them work in the earth-moving business. In Chapter 10 R.G. will face a major life-changing decision. He will make a decision on how best to serve God with his talents and passions.

What jobs are the best for honoring God?

How did passion help R.G. overcome difficult business situations?

What is more important when choosing a career: passion, path, or partnering with God?

Chapter 9 – 1919 (31 years old)
Historical Events in 1919:
- The 18th Amendment to the United States Constitution is ratified. (Prohibition)
- U.S. Congress establishes the Grand Canyon National Park.
- Treaty of Versailles ends World War I (June).
- U.S. Congress passes the Volstead Act to begin Prohibition (October).
- The Green Bay Packers are founded by Earl "Curly" Lambeau and George Whitney Calhoun.

Chapter 10 – 1919 to 1920 (32 years old)
Historical Events in 1919: (continued)
- U.S. Marines invade Costa Rica (June) and then Honduras (September).
- Woodrow Wilson wins the 1919 Nobel Peace Prize (awarded in 1920).
Historical Events in 1920:
- First radio news program is broadcast.
- Water skiing is invented in France.
- The first transatlantic two-way radio is broadcast.
- The 19th Amendment to the United States Constitution is ratified. (Women's Suffrage)

Watch for these Key Words: debt, scrapper, Christmas, businessmen

Study 5

Chapter 9 – 1919

1. What were the terms R.G. agreed to for selling his half of the garage? (Page 92, Projects)

   Honest self-assessment: *"I was 30 years old, unemployed, and $5,000 in debt."* (Page 92)

2. What happened the next day that started R.G. in the earth-moving business? (Pages 92-93, Partnering)

3. How was R.G. able to raise $400 to buy the Saxon automobile? (Page 94, Path)

4. How did R.G. benefit from the broken-down scrapper? (Pages 95-96, Passion)

5. What was the weakness of all tractor-drawn scrappers? (Pages 96-97, Passion)

6. What did the sign on the safety bulletin board say about experience? (Page 98, Projects)

7. Summarize the development of the Caterpillar tractor. (Pages 101-102, Passion)

8. Why will they "never forget the Christmas of 1919"? (Page 104, Path)

Study 5

Chapter 10 – 1919 to 1920

9. List some of the disadvantages of using mules. (Page 106, Passion)

10. What was Sarah's challenge to R.G.? (Page 108, Path)

11. After he committed himself to doing God's work, what message did he receive? (Page 109, Partnering)

12. What did R.G. think it meant to serve the Lord? (Page 110, Partnering)

13. How did R. G. get into the land-leveling business? (Pages 110-111, Path)

14. What improvements did R.G. invent for the scraper as he rode on the "thinking seat" of the old Holt? (Pages 111-112, Passion)

15. How much additional salary do you get for the "man who isn't there"? (Page 113, Projects)

Study 5

Secrets in Scripture

*And working together with Him, we also urge you not to receive the grace of God in vain--
for He says, "AT THE ACCEPTABLE TIME I LISTENED TO YOU, AND ON THE
DAY OF SALVATION I HELPED YOU." Behold, now is "THE ACCEPTABLE
TIME," behold, now is "THE DAY OF SALVATION."*

2 Corinthians 6:1-2 (NASB)

What are some of the ways we can "work together" with God?

How do we "work against" God?

What happens if we accept God's grace and do not share it with others?

*Then He said to His disciples, "The harvest is plentiful, but the workers are few.
Therefore beseech the Lord of the harvest to send out workers into His harvest."*

Matthew 9:37-38 (NASB)

Secrets of Success

Insight into the truths of mechanical engineering:
"In mechanics a nice feature is that once you have found the cause of the trouble, the cure is usually simple – if you have found the right cause." (Page 100)

What does it mean to have complete faith in God?
"You know, a lot of people take their problems to the Lord, and get up and walk away, carrying their problems back with them … The Lord can't help you if you insist on carrying your problems with you. Leave them with Him, and they are no longer yours but His." (Page 103)

Is this still true today?
"Man is worth what a man produces, and when machines increase his production he is worth more. The reason we have the highest standards of living in the world is because we are the most mechanized country in the world so our production per man is highest." (Page 113)

R.G. LeTourneau with George H. W. Bush

George Bush was then President of the Zapata Offshore Company

Photograph courtesy of R.G. LeTourneau Heritage Center

"Full-Drag Scraper" built in 1921

This is the first scraper ever built by R.G. LeTourneau

Photograph courtesy of R.G. LeTourneau Heritage Center

Study 6

Looking Back

1920 was a difficult business year for R.G. He had lost money on several ventures, including the leaking cement pipe project. And, yet, his mindset was changing to consider the immaterial benefits as being greater than the material benefits. "Another year shot, and still just as much in debt as ever. In spite of the set-back, we found ourselves rich in the Lord's blessings." (Page 115)

Why is it so easy to focus on material things, and forget about immaterial things?

Do you expect that God's path for your life will include both good times, and challenging times?

Looking Ahead

The intensity of R.G.'s passion for his earth-moving machines meant that there was always room for improvement. His drive to develop more efficient machines meant that R.G. would spend many hours a day thinking of weaknesses that could be converted to strengths.

How can a weakness found in a machine be turned into a strength or selling point?

How do people often respond to their personal weaknesses?

Is it possible to turn a personal weakness into a personal strength?

Chapter 11 – 1921 (33 years old)

Historical Events in 1921:
- Warren Harding is inaugurated the 29th U.S. President.
- Oil is discovered near Long Beach, California.
- Albert Einstein wins the Nobel Prize for Physics.
- The first radio broadcast of a baseball game is aired in Pittsburgh, Pennsylvania.

Chapter 12 – 1922 to 1923 (34 to 35 years old)

Historical Events in 1922:
- The first paid radio commercials are broadcast.
- Sound-on-file motion pictures are demonstrated for the first time in the United States.
- Insulin is used for first time to treat diabetes.
- The Lincoln Memorial is dedicated.

Historical Events in 1923:
- The New York Yankees defeat the Boston Red Socks in the first game at Yankee Stadium.
- Time Magazine is published for the first time.
- Warren G. Harding dies and is succeeded by Calvin Coolidge (30th U.S. President).
- The Walt Disney Company is founded by Roy and Walt Disney.

Watch for these Key Words: employees, patents, Gondola, invention

Study 6

Chapter 11 – 1921

1. What were the purchase terms of their first "real home"? How did the home provide the facilities for R.G. LeTourneau, Inc.? (Pages 116-117, Path)

2. How did God provide work during the "famine" after losing a "winter's contract"? (Pages 117-118, Partnering)

3. Describe the growth of his first company, both employees and sales. (Pages 118-119, Projects)

4. Is it possible to start your own business today? What is the secret? (Pages 120-121, Projects)

5. Describe the oil drilling ventures. (Pages 120-121, Projects)
   (The president of the Zapata Offshore Company at that time was George H. W. Bush.)

6. What two things came out of the first scraper? (Page 122, Passion)

7. What insights about patents does R.G. share with his readers? (Page 123, also Page 125, Path)

Study 6

Chapter 12 – 1922 to 1923

8. Are there any more "worlds to conquer"? Why will that always be true? (Page 126, Projects)

9. What were the drawbacks of the Gondola? (Page 127, Passion)

10. What inspired R.G. to invent his next scraper? (Page 128, Passion)

11. How long did the Mountain Mover last? (Page 129, Passion)

12. What did R.G. use when he ran out of bronze? (Page 130, Projects)

13. What is the difference between "invention and development"? (Page 131, Projects)

14. What was the name of the third scraper, the one with electric wheels? (Page 132, Passion)

15. What was the result of Ira's comment? (Page 132, Path)

16. What kind of business did R.G. decide to enter? (Page 133, Projects)

Study 6

Secrets in Scripture

When R.G. experiences another low point, "I had to stand on tiptoe and reach up to touch bottom," God provided him a house for no money down. (Page 116)

What lesson do we learn about God's provision from the story below of the widow and her son?

> *But she said, "As the LORD your God lives, I have no bread, only a handful of flour in the bowl and a little oil in the jar; and behold, I am gathering a few sticks that I may go in and prepare for me and my son, that we may eat it and die." Then Elijah said to her, "Do not fear; go, do as you have said, but make me a little bread cake from it first and bring it out to me, and afterward you may make one for yourself and for your son. For thus says the LORD God of Israel, `The bowl of flour shall not be exhausted, nor shall the jar of oil be empty, until the day that the LORD sends rain on the face of the earth.' " So she went and did according to the word of Elijah, and she and he and her household ate for many days. The bowl of flour was not exhausted nor did the jar of oil become empty, according to the word of the LORD which He spoke through Elijah.*
>
> 1 Kings 17:12-16 (NASB)

Secrets of Success

Encouraging words to "young" people:

"… the young man of today is far better trained to start a business such as mine than I was. The point they miss in their impatience is that I didn't start a big business. It may sound like an exaggeration, but I was in my business for five years before I noticed it had started. It was that small." (Page 121)

"I've heard young engineers in my own shop complain that they've arrived too late to make any major discoveries. That's all nonsense. All inventors stand on the shoulders of the inventors who have gone before them, and the bigger the inventors, the higher the newcomers can stand." (Page 126)

Constantly looking for ways to make improvements:

"I've heard it called both efficiency and laziness, but when I start a job I instinctively hunt for the easiest way and then, mindful of Mr. Hill in Portland, the fastest way." (Page 114)

Moss Ave 1, Stockton, California

Photograph courtesy of R.G. LeTourneau Heritage Center

R.G. LeTourneau - 1927

Photograph courtesy of R.G. LeTourneau Heritage Center

Study 7

Looking Back

After several years building earth-moving equipment, R.G. decided to enter into a new business arena. "If no one wanted to buy my untested earth-moving machines, I would enter the heavy construction business, and test the machines myself." (Page 133)

What were some of the machines R.G. had developed by this time in his life?

Why do you think it would be a challenging transition from machine production to construction?

Looking Ahead

As the business grows, so does the size of the machines, and the complexity of the projects. R.G. has a foot in two worlds. On one hand he is designing and building huge earth-moving equipment. On the other hand he will be overseeing huge earth-moving projects.

Up to this point we have seen many events in R.G.'s life that prepared him for the design and production of earth-moving equipment. What events helped prepare him for project management?

Which requires better people skills, building equipment or managing projects?

Chapter 13 – 1924 to 1925 (36 to 37 years old)
Historical Events in 1924:
- Clarence Birdseye invents a process for producing quick-frozen food.
- Chamonix, France hosts the first Olympic winter games.
- Native Americans proclaimed U.S. Citizens by the "Indian Citizenship Act of 1924."
Historical Events in 1925:
- Chrysler Corporation is founded by Walter Percy Chrysler.
- John T. Scopes is tried for teaching evolution in a Tennessee high school in violation of the state's Butler Act.
- F. Scott Fitzgerald publishes "The Great Gatsby."

Chapter 14 – 1926 to 1927 (38 to 39 years old)
Historical Events in 1926:
- The aerosol spray can is invented by Erik Rotheim, a Norwegian chemical engineer.
- Robert Goddard launches the first liquid-propellant rocket in Auburn, Massachusetts.
- NBC radio network begins with 24 stations.
Historical Events in 1927:
- The first transatlantic telephone call is made between New York City and London.
- Lindbergh completes the first solo non-stop transatlantic flight.
- Al Jolson stars in "The Jazz Singer."

Watch for these Key Words: pipeline, hillside, Henry Kaiser, excuses

Study 7

Chapter 13 – 1924 to 1925

1. What was R.G.'s unique approach to keeping his employees? (Page 134, Projects)

2. What kind of men would R.G. try to hire? (Page 135, Projects)

3. What did R.G. pick to give Evelyn some relief? (Page 136, Projects)

4. What was the solution R.G. developed for working on the steep hillside? (Page 137, Passion)

5. What were the advantages of the bulldozer blade developed for Crow Canyon? (Page 140, Passion)

6. Who was Henry Kaiser and why was he important? (Pages 141-142, Projects)

Study 7

Chapter 14 – 1926 to 1927

7. When evaluating future projects, what tendency keeps planners from moving ahead? (Page 143, Projects)

8. Similar to the winding path of R.G.'s life, Kaiser had many experiences before they met. List the jobs Kaiser had before getting into contracting. (Pages 143-144, Path)

9. Instead of "trick instruments to do small jobs faster," how did Kaiser see the earth-movers? (Page 144, Projects)

10. What was the milestone reached at Philbrook Dam? (Page 145, Projects)

11. When R.G. started to make excuses or blame others, what was Kaiser's response? (Page 146, Path)

12. Once you "realize your troubles are your own," what should you do next? (Page 147, Partnering)

13. What was the deal Kaiser made for the factory? Why did he buy all the machinery? (Pages 148-149, Projects)

14. What happened to the hoppers in Mississippi that caused a rift between R.G. and Kaiser? (Page 153, Projects)

Study 7

Secrets in Scripture

Divided attention is a recipe for an accident. "Watch the road when you drive." "Pay attention in class." "Aim carefully before you pull the trigger."

What do the following verses teach us about maintaining a partnership with God?

"No one can serve two masters; for either he will hate the one and love the other, or he will be devoted to one and despise the other. You cannot serve God and wealth."
Matthew 6:24 (NASB)

The house of the wicked will be destroyed,
But the tent of the upright will flourish.
There is a way which seems right to a man,
But its end is the way of death.
Proverbs 14:11-12 (NASB)

What are some possible outcomes to seeking first God's kingdom, but having other kingdoms that we are also seeking?

Secrets of Success

More thoughts on constantly looking for ways to make improvements:
"The general idea of building big machines is to turn them loose on bigger jobs. The fact is, there are no big jobs; only small machines … Yet the tendency is still strong to measure future jobs on the basis of past experience instead of modern machinery." (Page 143)

Learning from circumstances and mistakes:
"Well, now, Bob," he said, "when things haven't gone as well as they probably should have, and you start to blame circumstances and other people instead of yourself, you are never going to improve. It's when you start to improve these matters yourself that you improve the matters and yourself both." (Henry Kaiser, Page 146)

"… when a man admits his mistakes and is willing to learn from them with the Lord's help, new worlds can open up." (Page 154)

Why do people have so much trouble admitting their own mistakes?

"I was amazed and a bit puzzled. But when I thought things through I saw that this man was clever. He wasn't going to have me working for him by day, and then going home to do jobs for myself in my own workshop. He wanted all there was of me, so he bought me right out. And that' show God wants us to serve Him. The Bible says 'no man can serve two masters,' but the trouble with so many Christian people is that they are trying to do just that. And, it's won't work."

R.G. LeTourneau reflecting on the offer by Henry Kaiser to buy the entire company.

Ackland, Donald F. *Moving Heaven and Earth*.
New York: The Iversen-Ford Associates, 1949, Page 183

"Some people say that religion and business won't mix. Well, they used to say that oil and water won't mix either, but in our manufacturing plants where we operate a lot of machine tools we use thousands of gallons of oil and water for cooling the tools as they run at high speed. It is a white mixture that looks like milk, but actually it is oil and water with a third ingredient added that causes the oil and water to mix. Religion and business will mix when the Lord Jesus Christ enters the human heart."

R.G. LeTourneau answering a question about mixing religion with business.

Lorimer, Albert W. *God Runs My Business: The Story of R.G. LeTourneau*.
New York: Fleming H. Revell Company, 1941, Pages 174

R.G. LeTourneau Discussing a Design with an Engineer

Photograph courtesy of R.G. LeTourneau Heritage Center

Study 8

Looking Back

"Mistakes are to be avoided at all cost." Or, "if you never make mistakes you will never learn." There are many famous quotations about making mistakes. On one hand, no one wants to experience the disappointment and frustration which accompany failure. On the other side, as pointed out by Mr. Kaiser, God can work through our mistakes if we trust in His guidance.

What are some lessons R.G. has learned from his mistakes over the years?

Give an example of an improvement R.G. made to one of his machines to correct a shortcoming.

Looking Ahead

In many ways R.G. was a one person production and construction company. He could design, and improve his own machines. He modified his machines to meet the requirements of a new project. And, yet, at every step you see R.G. included many people in all of his business ventures. In the next two chapters, you will see how R.G. builds an entire construction camp to provide resources for his projects.

What kind of employees does R.G. need for his business? Consider both labor skills and work ethic.

What is the most important part of the team, the coach or the players?

Chapter 15 – 1928 (40 years old)
Historical Events in 1928:
- The Summer Olympics are held in Amsterdam, Netherlands.
- "Plane Crazy," the first Mickey Mouse animation, is released by Disney Studios.
- Amelia Earhart becomes the first woman to fly across the Atlantic Ocean.
- The Boulder Dam Act authorized the construction of a dam and power plant in either Boulder or Black Canyon.

Chapter 16 – 1929 (41 years old)
Historical Events in 1929:
- St. Valentine's Day Massacre results in the death of seven gangsters in Chicago.
- The first Academy Awards are held in Hollywood, California.
- The San Francisco Bay Toll-Bridge opens linking the San Francisco Peninsula with the East Bay.
- Herbert Hoover is inaugurated as the 31st U.S. president.
- The first public demonstration of color television is presented by Bell Telephone Laboratories in New York.
- The U.S. stock market reaches a new high on September 3.
- The U.S. stock market collapses during the "Wall Street Crash of 1929," October 24 to 29.

Watch for these Key Words: diesel, rack and pinion, Russia, Los Angeles

Study 8

Chapter 15 – 1928

1. What was the big advantage R.G. had over his competition? (Page 155, Projects)

2. What was the challenge of the Patterson Ditch? (Pages 155-156, Projects)

3. With the new jobs coming in, R.G. needed machines. What was his "most serious problem"? (Page 158, Projects)

4. What was the problem with the diesel engines used "up there in Eureka"? (Page 158, Passion)

5. What did R.G. learn while he was asking God for help? (Pages 158-159, Partnering)

6. Instead of rack and pinion gears, what was R.G.'s new solution? (Page 159, Passion)

7. Describe the work process between R.G. and his engineers. (Pages 159-160, Projects)

8. Why was the L & L Construction Company formed? How did it work out? (Pages 161–163, Projects)

9. What happens when you put your confidence in God? When you don't? (Pages 165-168, Partnering)

Study 8

Chapter 16 – 1929

10. In spite of the crash on Wall Street, why was 1929 significant to R.G.? (Page 169, Projects)

11. Describe a typical construction camp. (Page 170, Projects)

12. Why did R.G. build and maintain his own equipment? (Page 170, Projects)

13. What were some of the issues raised by the potential to sell to Russia? (Pages 170-171, Projects)

14. What were some of the improvements of the new factory? (Pages 171-172, Projects)

15. Why was the new factory built in Stockton, instead of Los Angeles? (Page 172, Path)

16. Describe the faith of "true Christians" as opposed to "a man of little faith." (Page 173, Partnering)

Study 8

Secrets in Scripture
In the middle of Newhall Cut-off project, R.G. was given a chance to bid on the Suison Bay railroad bridge. He recalls that "the Lord invites us to prove Him." (Page 163)

Why are we afraid to prove God?

What does it show when we withhold some of the tithe?

Why might it be difficult for a farmer to give the whole tithe before he has gathered the entire harvest?

> *"Bring the whole tithe into the storehouse, so that there may be food in My house, and test Me now in this," says the LORD of hosts, "if I will not open for you the windows of heaven and pour out for you a blessing until it overflows."*
>
> Malachi 3:10 (NASB)

Secrets of Success
Giving a "first fruit" offering is something difficult to understand in the "digital age." For the ancient farmer it meant giving the first of the harvest to God. This act takes faith because harvest time may come only once a year. It takes faith because there is no guarantee the rest of the produce will be gathered before it is ruined. The statement made by a "first fruit" offering is one of trusting God to provide, and not trusting in the soil, the sun, or the weather.

"Let God's will be done, and the rewards will be so great there won't be room to store them. But start to hedge, and wait to see how the whole crop turns out before giving God His share, and he knows you as a man of little faith." (Page 173)

Most people today do not depend on harvesting a crop for their food or their income. Instead, it is often easy to buy items with a credit card, even if we do not have the money at that time.

How can businesspeople today demonstrate faith through a "first fruits" offering?

Corporal Missile Erector

Photograph courtesy of R.G. LeTourneau Heritage Center

Power Control Unit (PCU)

This design was created after the meeting at the Peniel Mission. (Pages 194–195)

Photograph courtesy of R.G. LeTourneau Heritage Center

Study 9

Looking Back
The Great Depression started in 1929 with the stock market crash and leading to the failure of many banks. Even during this extremely difficult time R.G. remained faithful to God. And, God blessed R.G. and his business.

In what ways is the current economic situation similar to the Great Depression?

In what ways is the current economic condition different from the Great Depression?

Looking Ahead
Overcoming big obstacles was a big part of R.G.'s life and his success. As you consider the next two chapters, pay attention to all the obstacles that R.G. faced, and conquered.

How did R.G.'s faith in God help him to overcome obstacles?

What are some positive steps people can take when they are facing daunting challenges?

Chapter 17 – 1930 to 1931 (42 to 43 years old)
Historical Events in 1930:
- Gandhi leads a civil disobedience campaign in India.
- Japan invades Manchuria.
- Construction is completed of the Chrysler Building in New York City.
- German scientists Walther Bothe and Herbert Becker observe a new form of penetrating radiation.
- Scotch Cellulose Tape is invented by a 3M engineer, Richard Drew.
- Twinkies are invented by a bakery manager, James Dewar, in Schiller Park, Illinois.
Historical Events in 1931:
- Construction of the Empire State Building is completed and work on the Rockefeller Center starts.
- The Chinese Soviet Republic is proclaimed by Mao Zedong.
- The Star-Spangled Banner becomes the National Anthem of the United States.

Chapter 18 – 1932 (44 years old)
Historical Events in 1932:
- Hattie W. Caraway becomes the first U.S. woman Senator.
- Veterans of World War I, the Bonus Army, march on Washington D.C.
- U.S. unemployment increases to 24 %. (From 1932 into 1935 unemployment was above 20 %.)
- The first gas tax in the United States is enacted through the "Revenue Act of 1932."
- James Chadwick identifies the radiation found by Bothe and Becker as the neutron.

Watch for these Key Words: black stratum, loyal, pencil, vicious circle

Study 9

Chapter 17 – 1930 to 1931

1. What "gave urgency" to the highway R.G. was to build? (Page 174, Path)

2. What was the problem with black stratum, and how was it solved? (Pages 175–177, Passion)

3. Why is it that no manufacturer can make the perfect proving grounds? (Page 177, Projects)

4. What deal did R.G. work out with the State Inspector of Dams? (Page 179, Projects)

5. What did R.G. see as "an extravagantly wasteful use of human lives"? (Page 180, Passion)

6. What caused Mr. Hall to change his mind? (Page 183, Partnering)

7. According to R.G., when can the Lord lead us? (Page 188, Partnering)

Study 9

Chapter 18 – 1932

8. Describe the "first big break" and the benefits of this breakthrough. (Pages 190-191, Projects)

9. What two things happened that allowed R.G. to make payroll and meet his pledge? (Page 192, Projects)

10. List the profits from 1930, 1931, and 1932. Remember, these were the years of the "Great Depression." (Page 193, Partnering)

11. Describe the improvements in the "Carryall scraper." (Page 193, Passion)

12. Why is it folly to put your "own problems ahead of the Lord's work"? (Page 194, Partnering)

13. List the four elements found in the "vicious circle of big industry." (Page 196, Projects)

Study 9

Secrets in Scripture

R.G. states that "we need to walk softly before the Lord, and be sure it isn't our own desires that we mistake for the Lord's voice." (Page 188)

> *Trust in the LORD with all your heart*
> *And do not lean on your own understanding.*
> *In all your ways acknowledge Him,*
> *And He will make your paths straight.*

Proverbs 3:5-6 (NASB)

Why do we tend to lean on our own understanding?

Why can't the Lord lead us if we do not trust Him with all our heart?

What do you think it means for the Lord to make our "paths straight"?

Secrets of Success

Keys to Good Management:

- Understanding the viewpoint of others:
    "I realized his position." (Page 179)

- Doing the hard work up front:
    "The first month of getting organized on a job is always the hardest …" (Page 179)

- Involving and valuing the opinions of others:
    "I called in my key men … 'Think we can do it?'" (Page 180)

- Managing workflow:
    "They had to time the job so that no one machine or crew would be held up by another." (Page 180)

- Results in customer, employee loyalty:
    "I had a mighty loyal bunch of men." (Page 180)

"I believe my Bible and I believe the story of creation because it is a reasonable explanation of things. Look at my by 300 horse-power *Tournapull*. Could anyone be so silly as to think that it just happened like that? Of course not. So, when we look at the world, we know that there must have been a Mind and a Maker behind it."

R.G. LeTourneau speaking to the staff at the Peoria Plant.

Ackland, Donald F. *Moving Heaven and Earth.*
New York: The Iversen-Ford Associates, 1949, Page 188

"In making this report to a world that is bleeding and torn with hatred, strife, and selfishness, it might be well to remember that spiritual things are worth more than material things. Jesus said, 'Lay up for yourselves treasures in heaven.'"

"I love Him because He suffered for me, and I am trying to serve him, not just so He will take me to heaven when I die, but because I have caught a vision of His marvelous program, and I want to take part in that Program both here and hereafter."

R.G. LeTourneau from the "President's Personal Message," in his 1940 annual report.

Lorimer, Albert W. *God Runs My Business: The Story of R.G. LeTourneau.*
New York: Fleming H. Revell Company, 1941, Page 107

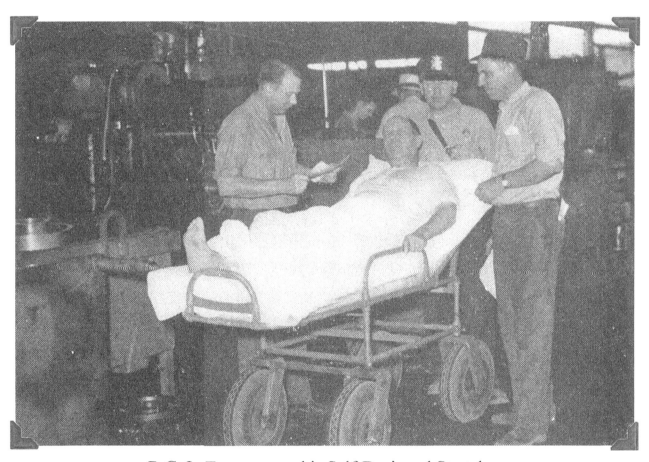

R.G. LeTourneau on his Self-Designed Stretcher

"The first machine I designed was a stretcher on which I could be
wheeled through the factory on inspection tours." (Page 214)

Photograph courtesy of R.G. LeTourneau Heritage Center

Study 10

Looking Back
One of the main themes of his autobiography is R.G.'s life path. He knew God had directed his life at many different times, in many different ways, to prepare him for many different challenges. R.G. also often acknowledged how God used other people in his life to assist, provide experience, and even cause adversity.

Refer back to Chapter 18 and see if you can find these people who influenced R.G.'s life and decisions: Nick Basich, Bill LeTourneau, Denn Burgess, Evelyn LeTourneau, Ken Parks, and Carlton Case

Looking Ahead
People who have heard of R.G. LeTourneau most likely have heard about his commitment to giving to God's work. In Chapter 19 R.G. tells the story to how Evelyn influenced him as they made a truly staggering commitment.

Do you find it easy or difficult to give money that you have earned to God?

How should people decide how much money to give to God?

Chapter 19 – 1933 to 1934 (45 to 46 years old)
Historical Events in 1933:
- Franklin D. Roosevelt becomes the 32nd President of the United States.
- The Civil Works Administration, the Civilian Conservation Corps, and the Tennessee Valley Authority are formed.
- Construction begins on the Golden Gate Bridge in San Francisco.
- A strong dust storm strips topsoil in South Dakota during the "Dust Bowl."
- Prohibition is repealed by the 21st Amendment.

Historical Events in 1934:
- The Securities and Exchange Commission is created by the Securities Exchange Act.
- Adolf Hitler becomes "Fuehrer" in Germany.
- The first All-American Soap Box Derby is held in Dayton, Ohio.

Chapter 20 – 1935 to 1936 (47 to 48 years old)
Historical Events in 1935:
- Amelia Earhart flies solo from Honolulu, Hawaii to Oakland, California.
- Alcoholics Anonymous is founded by Bill Wilson and Dr. Bob Smith.
- President Roosevelt signs the Social Security Act.
- The Monopoly board game is released by Parker Brothers.

Historical Events in 1936:
- Arabs revolt against the British in Palestine.
- The Summer Olympics are held in Berlin, Germany.
- The novel "Gone with the Wind" is published.

Watch for these Key Words: Peoria, LeTourneau Foundation, vocational, head on

Study 10

Chapter 19 – 1933 to 1934

1. What were some of the advantages of rubber tires compared to steel wheels? (Pages 197-198, Passion)

2. Why did the operators change in response to the low-pressure air tires? (Page 199, Projects)

3. 1933 and 1934 were some of the worst years of the "Great Depression." How were R.G.'s sales and profits during these years? (Page 199, Partnering)

4. Why did they move the manufacturing to Peoria, Illinois? (Page 200, Projects)

5. How long did it take to get the new plant operating on the first scrapers? (Page 201, Projects)

6. Describe the role Evelyn played in the supporting the production workers. (Page 201, Path)

7. In his first speech to the Peoria Chamber of Commerce, how did R.G. describe the responsibility of Christian businessmen? (Page 203, Partnering)

8. How much of the company profits were given to the foundation? Personal income? (Pages 204-205, Partnering)

9. "When the Lord gives you a job to do, He'll give you the _____ and the _____ to do it." (Page 206, Partnering)

Study 10

Chapter 20 – 1935 to 1936

10. Why did R.G. start his first training program? (Page 207, Path)

11. What other classes were added to the "vocational school"? (Page 208, Project)

12. What is "*Now*," and how did it get started? (Page 208, Partnering)

13. Why was it important that R.G. accepted speaking invitations? (Page 211, Partnering)

14. What were the advantages and disadvantages of depending on trains to get to speaking engagements? (Page 211, Projects)

15. May 30, 1937 was another close call for R.G. How did he react to the accident? (Page 213, Partnering)

16. Why didn't the doctors want to start surgery on R.G.? (Page 214, Pain)

17. What two machines did R.G. design once he was released from the hospital? (Page 214, Passion)

Study 10

<u>Secrets in Scripture</u>
At the end of Chapter 20, R.G. writes about suffering tremendous physical pain and personal loss. He recalls that he responded by referring to the suffering of Job.

How can physical pain help us to draw near to God?

> *Then Job answered the LORD and said, "I know that You can do all things,*
> *And that no purpose of Yours can be thwarted ... I have heard of You by the*
> *hearing of the ear; But now my eye sees You ..."*
>
> Job 42: 1, 5 (NASB)

Shortly after the accident R.G. expressed confidence in God as he remembered this verse:

> *And we know that God causes all things to work together for good to those who love God,*
> *to those who are called according to His purpose.*
>
> Romans 8:28 (NASB)

Which is more difficult for you, to trust God in difficult situations, or to trust God when everything is going great?

Secrets of Success
Partnership in marriage:
"Through all this, Evelyn was right with me. I remember the day some industrialists' wives came to call to welcome her to Peoria. She was down at the factory site, using the family Chevrolet to snake steel beams off a flat car so we could clear the track for another trainload of steel." (Page 201)

Partnership in giving:
"In the old days a tithe was forced on people, and they had to give ten per cent of their income to God whether they wanted to or not. Now we aren't compelled to give to God. It's all voluntary." (Page 204)

Partnering with your employees by caring for their emotional and spiritual welfare:
"If the men in the armed services needed spiritual advisers and showed no hesitancy about admitting it, why should the men in industry supporting the armed forces be denied the same aid?" (Page 210)

Toccoa Tournapull #4

Photograph Courtesy of R.G. LeTourneau Heritage Center

LeTourneau Equipment Landing on the Beach in WWII

Photograph courtesy of R.G. LeTourneau Heritage Center

Study 11

Looking Back

On April 1, 1935 "a freight train with machine tools, and with about 75 key men started for Peoria…" The LeTourneau equipment company was on the move. God was moving in R.G.'s life, too. Speaking engagements were increasing, *Now* was being published on a regular basis, and the first vocational school was open.

Looking Ahead

While recovering from the injuries he received in the tragic automobile accident, R.G. continues to design and improve his machines. While facing his personal physical challenges, R.G. and his company will soon face the harsh reality of World War II.

In Study 1 we saw how R.G.'s stubborn streak caused tension with his father. How is this stubborn streak beneficial while R.G. faces multiple business and technical challenges?

Chapter 21 – 1937 to 1939 (49 to 51 years old)
Historical Events in 1937:
- Japan invades China (start of World War II in Asia) and slaughters 300,000 in Nanjing.
- Walt Disney's first full length animation movie is released, "Snow White and the Seven Dwarfs."

Historical Events in 1938:
- The "Munich Agreement," is signed by German, Italian, British and French leaders.
- Roy J. Plunkett of DuPont accidentally discovers polytetrafluoroethylene (Teflon).

Historical Events in 1939:
- The movies "Wizard of Oz" and "Gone with the Wind" are released.
- The United Kingdom, France, South Africa, Canada, New Zealand and Australia declare war on Germany.

Chapter 22 – 1940 to 1945 (52 to 57 years old)
Historical Events in 1940:
- The first McDonald's opens in San Bernardino, California.
- Winston Churchill becomes Prime Minister of the United Kingdom.

Historical Events in 1941:
- Glenn T. Seaborg discovers plutonium.
- The Imperial Japanese Navy attacks Pearl Harbor, killing over 2,400 people.

Historical Events in 1942:
- The first undersea oil pipeline is developed in an effort to provide oil to Allied forces on the European continent.
- In the Battle of Stalingrad forces from Russia resist and ultimately stop the eastern progress the German army.

Historical Events in 1943:
- "Oklahoma!" opens on Broadway.
- The Allied invasion of Sicily begins.

Historical Events in 1944:
- The D-Day Invasion on June 6 begins the Allied liberation of Western Europe.
- The first program-controlled calculator is built by IBM and installed at Harvard University.

Historical Events in 1945:
- Allied forces accept the unconditional surrender of Nazi Germany on May 8 (V-E Day).
- Japan formally surrenders aboard the battleship USS Missouri on September 2 (V-J Day).

Watch for these Key Words: Toccoa, friction, Hickam Field, Vicksburg

Study 11

Chapter 21 – 1937 to 1939

1. What was so unique about the Tournapull? (Pages 215-216, Passion)

2. What is "one of the first principles of engineering"? (Page 215, Passion)

3. What was the reaction of the Caterpillar company president to the Tournapull? (Page 216, Projects)

4. How did R.G. respond to "suppliers telling me to conform with their products"? (Page 217, Projects)

5. Since "the best is none too good," how did R.G. react to mass produced parts? (Pages 217-218, Projects)

7. Describe the progress of the LeTourneau foundation and Evelyn's contributions. (Page 219, Path)

8. What was the history and educational philosophy of the Toccoa Falls Institute? (Pages 219-220, Path)

9. Describe the machine R.G. designed to build concrete houses in Toccoa. (Page 221, Passion)

10. What is the "chief enemy of the mechanic"? (Page 223, Passion)

11. Do you agree with R.G. regarding the causes of World War II? (Pages 223-224, Partnering)

Study 11

Chapter 22 – 1940 - 1945

12. How did the Tournapulls display their value at Hickam Field? (Page 225, Passion)

13. What was "the greatest dirt-moving project the world has ever seen"? (Page 226, Projects)

14. How did the death of his oldest son, Donald, inspire R.G.? (Pages 226-227, Pain)

15. What two key elements were in short supply for R.G.'s factories? (Page 227, Projects)

16. How did R.G. respond to flooding and other obstacles at his new site on the Mississippi? (Pages 228-229, Projects)

17. After Vicksburg, where was the next LeTourneau production facility built? (Page 230, Path)

18. What was unusual about the airport at Bone, in North Africa? (Page 231, Projects)

19. List some of the ways earth-moving equipment served in World War II. (Pages 231-232, Projects)

20. What did R.G. do so that they would not "profit on what was a world catastrophe"? (Page 233, Partnering)

Study 11

Secrets in Scripture

What happens when leaders of countries set themselves up as "gods in their own right, super-beings who would lead the way with no need for God's guidance"? (Page 224)

Give some modern day examples of rulers or leaders who have set themselves up as someone not needing God's direction.

The fool has said in his heart, "There is no God." They are corrupt, they have committed abominable deeds; There is no one who does good. The LORD has looked down from heaven upon the sons of men to see if there are any who understand, Who seek after God. They have all turned aside, together they have become corrupt; There is no one who does good, not even one.

Psalm 14:1-3 (NASB)

Rulers who think they are "gods in their own right" would benefit from the words of King Nebuchadnezzar, the ruler of ancient Babylon, regarding the sovereignty of God:

His dominion is an eternal dominion; his kingdom endures from generation to generation. All the people of the earth are regarded as nothing. He does as he pleases with the powers of heaven and the people of the earth. No one can hold back his hand or say to him: "What have you done?"

Daniel 4:34-35 (NASB)

Secrets of Success

Strategy for designing equipment:
"Yet all I had done was obey one of the first principles of engineering. I had eliminated all unnecessary parts, and produced a machine that was stark in its simplicity." (Page 215)

Why would this strategy also work with human organizations?

In Chapter 3 R.G. declared that he was a "man growed" and would not attend the eighth grade. Later in life education and training became one of his passions. Skim from the bottom of page 219 to page 223 and note all of the references to education, students, training, etc.

What was R.G.'s philosophy of education and training for his employees?

R.G. LeTourneau Speaking - 1948

Photograph courtesy of R.G. LeTourneau Heritage Center

R.G. LeTourneau in Tournata, Liberia - March 1955

Photograph courtesy of R.G. LeTourneau Heritage Center

Study 12

Looking Back
During World War II the engineers and factories which produced LeTourneau equipment worked overtime to supply the needs of military forces in both Europe and the Pacific. With the end of the war R.G. remarked that there was a sudden decrease in demand for earth-moving equipment.

Why was earth-moving equipment so vital to the war effort?

Looking Ahead
The ability to adapt to ever-changing circumstances is vital in life and in business. In the aftermath of World War II the entire LeTourneau faces a completely different business environment. R.G. responds with his passion for machines and his project management experience to design and produce new machines for new assignments.

Electronic computers have only been in existence for about 80 years. How have computers and personal computing devices changed the world?

How have you personally benefitted from advancements in technology?

Chapter 23 – 1946 to 1950 (58 to 62 years old)
Historical Events in 1946:
- ENIAC, the first general-purpose computer is unveiled at the University of Pennsylvania.
- The first meeting of the United Nations General Assembly and Security Council is held in London, England.

Historical Events in 1947:
- The Truman Doctrine is announced by President Harry S. Truman.
- Jackie Robinson becomes the first African-American to play in a Major League Baseball game.

Historical Events in 1948:
- A Declaration of Independence is proclaimed in Israel.
- The United States launches the first monkey astronaut using a V2 rocket.

Historical Events in 1949:
- Israel becomes the 59th country admitted to the United Nations.
- Communist forces win the civil war in China and declare the existence of the People's Republic of China.

Historical Events in 1950:
- The North Korean People's Army invades South Korea and begins the Korean War.

Study 12: Chapter 24 – 1951 to 1952 (63 to 64 years old)
Historical Events in 1951:
- Chinese and North Korean troops recapture Seoul.
- William Shockley, John Bardeen, and Walter Brattain of Bell Labs announce the invention of the junction transistor.
- The Great Flood of 1951 in the Midwestern U.S. causes $935,000,000 worth of damage and kills 28 people.

Historical Events in 1952:
- For the first time, a mechanical heart is connected to a patent for 50 minutes during heart surgery.
- Dwight D. Eisenhower wins the U.S. presidential election.

Watch for these Key Words: lumber, Harmon Hospital, raw material, Liberia

Study 12

Chapter 23 – 1946 to 1950

1. What shortage encouraged R.G. to pursue pulpwood production? (Pages 234-235, Projects)

2. Describe a few of the "machines in need of an inventor" that R.G. designed for lumber work. (Page 236, Passion)

3. What were some of the areas of infrastructure that needed to be remade after the war? (Page 237, Projects)

4. How did the war change the expectations of contractors and "service-trained engineers"? (Page 237, Projects)

5. When they needed another factory, what were some of the key qualifications? (Pages 239-240, Projects)

6. What vision did the Lord show R.G. and Evelyn for the Harmon Hospital? (Pages 240-241, Partnering)

7. What were the distinctive aspects of this education project? (Pages 241-242, Path)

8. R.G. purchased a surplus Douglas A-26 bomber after World War II. How did he use his new "perfect environment"? (Page 244, Projects)

Study 12

Chapter 24 – 1951 to 1952

9. According to R.G., why did God give humans "raw materials"? (Page 245, Partnering)

10. Why are some areas that are rich in raw material poor economically? (Page 245, Projects)

11. Describe R.G.'s proposal and motivation for helping developing countries become more productive. (Page 246, Partnering)

12. What situation existed in Liberia? What did R.G. hear from "my Lord"? (Pages 247-248, Partnering)

13. R.G. saw opportunity in Liberia but also knew that before you can persuade people to change you have to first _____. (Page 249, Projects)

14. What are the elements of the four-point program? (Page 250, Projects)

15. R.G.'s idea of God is that of both _____ and _____. (Page 251, Partnering)

16. Machines should be used for the _____ ___ _____. (Page 251, Passion)

17. How did R.G. see his jungle clearing provide for the country? (Page 253, Partnering)

18. How would you describe the changes in people who were involved in the Tournata project? (Page 254, Projects)

Study 12

Secrets in Scripture

Chapter 23 ends with a proclamation of God's dominion over the earth and the air. How do you think R.G. was impacted throughout his life by an understanding of God's ownership of this world?

> *Then the Levites, Jeshua, Kadmiel, Bani, Hashabneiah, Sherebiah, Hodiah, Shebaniah and Pethahiah, said, "Arise, bless the LORD your God forever and ever! O may Your glorious name be blessed And exalted above all blessing and praise! You alone are the LORD. You have made the heavens, The heaven of heavens with all their host, The earth and all that is on it, The seas and all that is in them. You give life to all of them And the heavenly host bows down before You."*
>
> Nehemiah 9:5-6 (NASB)

> *The earth is the LORD'S, and all it contains, the world, and those who dwell in it. For He has founded it upon the seas and established it upon the rivers.*
>
> Psalm 24:1-2 (NASB)

Secrets of Success

"I am a designer of machines, and details like finance, advertising, and sales I prefer to leave in the hands of specialists in those fields. Every now and then, however, I am reminded that I am the president of the company as well as the designer, and then I have to back off, straighten my necktie, and size up the situation." (Page 238)

Three keys to success are given in this brief quote:
1. Know your strengths and your weaknesses.
2. Learn to team with people who are strong in areas where you are weak.
3. Know when and how to get involved when the situation requires more direct input.

Thoughts on recognizing God's gifts:
"God didn't have to give us wings to fly. He gave us the mechanical genius to fly further and faster than any winged creature in His realm, and as a mechanic, that is good enough for me." (Page 244)

"God gave us the raw materials to work with for nothing, and there is plenty to be had if we go to work and produce the things we want." (Page 245)

"Sno-Train" - Land Train Designed for Arctic Transportation

Photograph courtesy of R.G. LeTourneau Heritage Center

Billy Graham and R.G. LeTourneau - 1953

The structure behind them is a DOME that Mr. R.G. was building for Billy Graham. After its completion in Longview it was determined that Billy's organization couldn't use it, so it was never taken down. It became known in the Longview area as "The Billy Graham Tabernacle." It was estimated in 1954 to have a seating capacity of 12,000. It still stands today and is used in the manufacturing processes of LeTourneau Technologies.

Photograph and caption courtesy of R.G. LeTourneau Heritage Center

Study 13

Looking Back
Growing up in Duluth as a young boy, R.G. could have no idea of the amazing adventures that God had prepared for his life. He started businesses, manufacturing plants, and colleges in California, Illinois, Georgia, Australia, Mississippi, England, Liberia, Peru, and Texas.

Having read R.G.'s life story, in his own words, what do you think were the characteristics that God used to accomplish so much in one ordinary person?

Looking Ahead
Throughout the book R.G. has given insights into his philosophy of engineering. He has talked about designing equipment with paper and pencil, while driving tractors, while flying on an airplane, and while he lay on a hospital stretcher. He believed that God created man to create and to overcome obstacles. He believed in being involved in every aspect of product, from design to testing and delivery.

How can you develop your own ability to create, design, and build?

Is the age of invention coming to a close, or are there many more machines to be designed?

Chapter 25 – 1953 to 1958 (65 to 70 years old)
Historical Events in 1953:
- An Armistice is signed bringing a halt to military action in the Korean War. (No peace treaty was ever signed.)
- The first color television sets go on sale in the United States.

Historical Events in 1954:
- The USS Nautilus, the first nuclear-powered submarine, is launched in Groton, Connecticut.
- The phrase "under God" is added to the U.S. Pledge of Allegiance.

Historical Events in 1955:
- Over 28,000 attend a press preview day as Disneyland is opened in Anaheim, California.
- Rosa Parks is arrested in Montgomery, Alabama for refusing to give up her seat to a white person on a public bus.

Historical Events in 1956:
- "In God We Trust" becomes the United States national motto.
- The first Hard Disk Drive is announced by engineers at IBM.

Historical Events in 1957:
- The Hamilton Watch Company produces the first electric watch, and the Wham-O company produces the first Frisbee.
- The Soviet Union launches the first human-made object to orbit the earth, Sputnik 1.

Historical Events in 1958:
- In response to Sputnik 1, President Eisenhower signs the National Aeronautics and Space Act, creating NASA.
- The Recession of 1958 begins as the result of worldwide economic decline.

Chapter 26 – 1959 to 1964 (71 to 76 years old, Died June 1, 1969)
Historical Events in 1959:
- Fidel Castro becomes the Premier of Cuba.
- Alaska (49th) and Hawaii (50th) gain statehood.

Watch for these Key Words: factory, four-point, future, fellowship

Study 13

Chapter 25 – 1953 to 1958

1. The way R.G. looked at business, a factory was just a _____ _____. (Page 255, Projects)

2. What were the limitations placed on R.G. by the Westinghouse contract? (Page 256, Path)

3. Summarize R.G.'s response to the 5 years of restrictions on building earth-moving equipment. (Page 256, Path)

4. How did R.G. deal with the "non-homogeneous structure of the soil"? (Page 257, Passion)

5. Where was the "second big Four-point program"? (Pages 257-258, Partnering)

6. Describe some of the "bigger" machines needed for Tournavista. (Page 259, Passion)

7. What is your reaction to R.G. describing the jungle as a place of "extravagant wastefulness"? (Page 260, Projects)

8. Since he was a partner with God, did R.G. expect there would be no challenges or failures? (Page 261, Partnering)

9. What are two possible results of "costly experience"? (Page 262, Path)

10. What products were first into production after the 5 year waiting period? (Pages 264-265, Projects)

Study 13

Chapter 26 – 1959 to 1964

11. Why was R.G. not worried about the future? (Page 267, Partnering)

12. What future improvements did R.G. envision for his "overland train"? (Page 268, Passion)

13. Do you think modern improvements restrict or inspire future ideas? Give an example. (Page 269, Projects)

14. What are some of the improvements R.G. made to ocean-based equipment? (Pages 269-271, Passion)

15. What benefits did R.G. see in building bigger machines? (Page 271, Passion)

16. What benefits did R.G. see in machines that could serve more than one purpose? (Page 273, Passion)

17. How did R.G. define a "successful idea"? (Page 274, Projects)

18. What attitude did R.G. have towards old age? (Page 274, Path)

19. To end his writing R.G. talks about fellowship with God. How does fellowship with God compare to, or differ from, partnering with God? (Page 275, Partnering)

Study 13

Secrets in Scripture

At the end of Chapter 26, R.G. talks about having fellowship with God. He looks forward to the time when his physical body will be transformed to a heavenly body. R.G. quotes Philippians 3:21 which talks about this transformation. From the verses below describe God and our hope for heavenly fellowship in the future.

For our citizenship is in heaven, from which also we eagerly wait for a Savior, the Lord Jesus Christ; who will transform the body of our humble state into conformity with the body of His glory, by the exertion of the power that He has even to subject all things to Himself.

Philippians 3:20-21 (NASB)

"Do not let your heart be troubled; believe in God, believe also in Me. In My Father's house are many dwelling places; if it were not so, I would have told you; for I go to prepare a place for you. If I go and prepare a place for you, I will come again and receive you to Myself, that where I am, there you may be also."

John 14:1-3 (NASB)

Secrets of Success

Look at a piece of U.S. currency. Notice the phrase "In God We Trust."
How would you compare R.G.'s desire to <u>partner</u> with God with <u>trusting</u> in God?

What are some other things, people, or positions that compete with God for our trust?

These verses were two of R.G.'s favorites. Hopefully, throughout your life, you will remember to believe always, seek continually, and trust God completely.

"For God so loved the world, that He gave His only begotten Son, that whoever believes in Him shall not perish, but have eternal life."

John 3:16 (NASB)

"But seek first His kingdom and His righteousness, and all these things will be added to you."

Matthew 6:33 (NASB)

R.G. and Evelyn LeTourneau – 1940's

Photograph courtesy of R.G. LeTourneau Heritage Center

Recommended Resources for Additional Study

Moving Heaven and Earth
R.G. LeTourneau
Inventor, Designer, Manufacturer, Preacher
by Donald F. Ackland
The Iversen-Ford Associates, New York, 1949

God Runs My Business
The Story of R.G. LeTourneau
Farmhand, Foundry Apprentice, Master Molder, Garage Mechanic, Laborer, Inventor,
Manufacturer, Industrialist, Christian Business Man, and Lay Evangelist
by Albert W. Lorimer
Fleming H. Revell Company, New York, MCMXLI

LeTourneau Earthmovers
by Eric C. Orlemann
MBI Publishing Company, St. Paul, MN, 2001

R.G. LeTourneau Heavy Equipment
The Mechanical Drive Era 1921-1953
by Eric C. Orlemann
Iconografix, Hudson, Wisconsin, 2008

R.G. LeTourneau Heavy Equipment
The Electric Drive Era 1953-1970
by Eric C. Orlemann
Iconografix, Hudson, Wisconsin, 2009

R.G. LeTourneau Museum and Archives
LeTourneau University, Longview, Texas
http://www.letu.edu/_Academics/library/Museum/

You can see an aerial view of "The Billy Graham Tabernacle," and 4 additional domes, if you search Internet satellite maps for: 2401 South High Street, Longview, Texas 75602.

We hope you have been encouraged and strengthened through

A Passion for Partnering with God

Study Guide based on
Mover of Men and Mountains
The Autobiography of R.G. LeTourneau

Visit us at www.wisdomcriesout.com

Please send your comments or suggestions to
comments@wisdomcriesout.com

Also available from Wisdom Cries Out Publications:

Ready to Receive, Ready to Share
Leadership Lessons from Paul to Timothy and Titus

Strength to Lead, Courage to Follow
Leadership Lessons from Joshua

The Parables of Jesus
A New Perspective

Wisdom
The Next Step

The Full Armor of God
In Action

Made in the USA
Middletown, DE
21 March 2023